C000023691

THE LITTLE BOOK OF

MOON MAGIC

TERESA DELLBRIDGE

RIDER

1 3 5 7 9 10 8 6 4 2

Rider, an imprint of Ebury Publishing,
20 Vauxhall Bridge Road,
London SW1V 2SA

Rider is part of the Penguin Random House group of companies
whose addresses can be found at global.penguinrandomhouse.com

Penguin
Random House
UK

First published in Great Britain by Rider in 2003
This edition published in 2020

www.penguin.co.uk

A CIP catalogue record for this book is available from the British Library

ISBN 9781846046483

Printed and bound in Great Britain by Clays Ltd, Elcograf S.p.A.

MIX
Paper from
responsible sources
FSC® C018179

Penguin Random House is committed to a
sustainable future for our business, our readers
and our planet. This book is made from Forest
Stewardship Council® certified paper.

WELCOME TO THE LITTLE BOOK OF MOON MAGIC!

The Moon is our guide in the realms of
enchantment. Wise, gentle, fascinating
and eerie, she is Queen of the fluctuating
forces that govern our lives. Tuning into
the Moon helps us to harmonise with
our own instincts and natural rhythms.
Rediscover what the ancients knew well
— that the Moon rules magic ...

Teresa Dellbridge

THE MOON'S PHASES

Become well acquainted with the Moon by watching her phases and noting how you react to them, from New Moon through to Full, Waning and back to New again. It takes 29½ days for the Moon to pass through this cycle.

When the New Moon appears in the evening sky, you can cup the silver sickle in your right palm in the Northern Hemisphere or in your left in the Southern Hemisphere.

As the days progress the Moon rises later and later, and when she is full she rides high in the sky at midnight.

When the Moon is waning she can be seen in the small hours, gradually disappearing into the dawn.

The 'Dark of the Moon' is the time between the disappearance of the waning Moon and the reappearance of the New Moon, when the Moon cannot be seen.

The Moon becomes 'new' in the middle of her dark period. She is invisible at this time because she is too close to the Sun. We see the first sickle of New Moon as she begins to draw away from the Sun at the start of a fresh cycle.

The Moon always keeps the same side turned towards us — we never see her other face.

BEFRIENDING
THE MOON

Keep a lunar diary to discover how the
Moon affects your feelings and actions. In it,
note down your dreams, how your energy
levels fluctuate, your state of health, how
much you accomplish, your relationships
with others and anything else that seems
important. Make a special note of any
intuitive insights or paranormal events.

You may also like to record the reactions
of your partner, friends, children, pets and
even plants!

Keep an eye on newspaper headlines —
do these reflect the Moon's phases?

After a few months you will come to
sense the powers of the Moon and how
these powers affect not only you, but the
subtle energy-field that surrounds us all.
Then you will be better placed to use this
energy in your lunar magic.

STRANGE
MOONS

BLUE MOON is a rare event when a
Full Moon occurs twice in one month,
with the first Full Moon being right at the
beginning of the month. The term is also
used for a Full Moon occurring twice in a
row in the same sign of the Zodiac.

HARVEST MOON is the golden Full Moon that we see in September. At this time of year the Moon rises slowly, hanging close to the horizon for longer than usual. The atmosphere acts like a magnifying glass and makes the Moon look like a great amber balloon.

HUNTER'S MOON is similar, but refers to a Full Moon in October. Stags rut and there is increased animal activity in preparation for winter.

ECLIPSES occur when the Sun and Moon are in line with the Earth. A lunar eclipse only happens at Full Moon when the Earth gets between the Sun and Moon, and the Moon appears to turn blood red at midnight. A solar eclipse only happens at New Moon when the Moon gets between the Sun and Earth. Because the Moon is relatively small, solar eclipses are rarely total. Eclipses were regarded as evil portents in ancient times. The Australian Aborigines believe that an eclipse of the Moon means that someone on a journey has come to harm.

The Moon's phase and eclipses are noted in newspapers. See how the next eclipse makes you feel.

THE MOON
AND THE TIDES

The Moon has always been associated
with water; in fact, the Aztec words for
'water' and 'Moon' were interchangeable,
and even land-locked peoples have often
associated her with the fall of dew.

Although the ancient Greeks did not
understand gravity, they knew the Moon
caused the tides. Many ancient peoples
believed that the affairs of humans were
also tidal.

High tide arrives with the passage of the Moon overhead and another comes 12 hours 25 minutes later, when the Moon reaches the opposite point beneath the Earth.

'Spring tides' occur at New and Full Moon. Tides are higher when the Moon is closest to the Earth and also at the Equinoxes.

While it is unlikely that the gravity of the Moon could affect us directly, there is little doubt that our bodies are 'tidal' in a more subtle sense, for life responds to the Moon.

WEREWOLVES
AND VAMPIRES

A werewolf is a person who turns into a wolf when the Moon is full. Like many myths, this one has a basis in reality, for the Full Moon brings out the wild and instinctual in all of us. It is interesting that this 'lunar' creature can be killed only by a silver bullet – the Moon's metal.

Vampires cannot bear the light of the Sun, so must exist by that of the Moon. These mythical creatures embody deep symbolic and psychological meanings. One of the things the vampire represents is all that is pushed into the darkness, but which refuses to die.

Lunar wisdom teaches that we should open our hearts and our imaginations, not to judge but to understand. By being open and accepting, we can enable the things we fear to come out of the shadows, transform and be reborn, as the Moon is every month.

LIVING BY
THE MOON

Living by the Moon may mean that your life runs more smoothly and that you feel healthier and more energetic.

NEW MOON: make plans and new beginnings, or make a new start on an established project. Put new resolutions into practice.

WAXING MOON: now projects can get into their stride. Be careful of overdoing things. Direct your enthusiasm well. Get in touch with friends, be active. If you need to be on a 'build-up' diet, now is the best time for your body to absorb nutrients.

FULL MOON: bring things to fruition and abandon what isn't working. Parties, outings, events, cooking in bulk, love-fests – all go best now.

WANING MOON: analyse things, shed
the unnecessary, have a big sort-out.
A detox or reducing diet will work
best now.

DARK MOON: enjoy a few quiet days;
think, reflect and start to plan the next
month.

GARDENING BY THE MOON

Plant life responds to the Moon's phases – knowing about this will give you green fingers.

FIRST SICKLE: plant seeds, especially herbs.

WAXING MOON: sow seeds over large areas. Lay turf. Water with special care because now the take-up of fluids is at its best. Pick fruit and vegetables that you are going to eat straight away.

APPROACHING FULL MOON: if the weather has been dry, it's best to plant most seeds now. Water once more. Pick fruit — it will be succulent — also herbs and flowers. Add fertiliser.

JUST AFTER FULL MOON: plant root veggies like potatoes and carrots. Plant trees and any flowers except annuals.

WANING MOON: attack those weeds! Prune trees, mow the grass, start or increase your compost heap. Pick plants that need to be stored.

APPROACHING DARK MOON: spray fruit-trees and cut timber.

CELEBRATE
THE MOON!

🌙

Need an excuse for a party or outing? The
phases of the Moon can give you ideas.

NEW MOON is a great time for launching
a new project, meeting new friends, starting
a class or taking up a new sport or hobby.

FULL MOON is an exciting time for a
big get-together. Romances blossom and
everyone feels more hyped-up. Buy a big

bunch of flowers; pour yourself a glass of something delicious and toast the Moon. Go to a gig or concert and soak up the vibes.

WANING MOON is a wonderful sorting-out time. Get together with friends to weed gardens, strip wallpaper and have a quiet time chatting and relaxing into the evening with close companions.

DARK MOON is a quieter time. You may choose to spend it with your family or alone. Light a candle, burn some incense and reflect upon your life and your plans.

MOON-CHILDREN

Young children are fascinated by the
Moon and can learn about natural cycles
including the idea of death and rebirth
from watching her phases.

Celebrate the Full Moon with a party for
any children you know – or just for the
child in you! Have a cake with white icing
decorated with silver. Light a big, white
candle. Encourage your guests to talk

about the Moon, recite poetry, make up
stories and even dress up and dance
around the garden in the moonlight.

If you are good at crafts, make a
cardboard tiara with a circle bounded by
two crescents pointing opposite ways, to
represent the phases. Paint this with glue
and sprinkle on silver glitter.

Take it in turns to be Moon Monarch and
say a party piece.

KISS YOUR HAND
TO THE MOON

Kissing a hand to the Moon is an old custom for bringing luck. You can also make the ancient sign of the Horned God (consort of the Moon) by bunching your hand into a fist and then extending only your index and little fingers, so your hand looks like the head of a horned animal. Hold this up towards the Moon so she looks as if she is cradled between the 'horns'. This works best of all as a New Moon greeting – a little act of worship that you can follow by making a wish.

DRINK TO THE MOON!

Lemons are ruled by the Moon. Make your own fresh lemonade from organic lemons, using 4 lemons, 5½ oz (120g) golden caster sugar and 2 pints (1140ml) of spring water. Squeeze the juice from the washed lemons and put the empty rinds in a large bowl. Boil the spring water, pour it over the rinds and add the sugar. Let it cool, strain, add the juice and chill. Raise your glass and drink down the lunar magic!

MAKING MOON CAKES

You can make these little cakes to celebrate the Full Moon. Eat them with a glass of white wine or grape juice and some butter and jam.

You will need:110g (4oz) butter – softened, 225g (8oz) golden granulated caster sugar, 2 free range eggs, 275g (10oz) organic plain flour, 1 tsp baking powder, 1 tsp salt, 1½ tbsp organic honey,

1 tsp vanilla extract (natural), 1 tsp white wine or white grape juice, 2 tbsp quick oats.

Mix the butter, sugar, eggs, honey, vanilla and wine thoroughly together. Blend in the flour, baking powder, oats and salt. Cover and chill for an hour, to make the dough easier to handle. Pre-heat the oven to 400°F, 200°C. Roll the dough out to the thickness of 5cm and cut into Full-Moon shapes with a pastry cutter. Bake for 6–8 minutes, until pale gold in colour.

Delicious!

MOON MEAL
CELEBRATION

☾

Hold a banquet for family and friends to celebrate Full Moon. Choose a spread of lunar foods such as milk, cheese, honey, white grape juice, white wine, cucumber, lettuce, white meat such as chicken, seafood (especially crustaceans), white bread and boiled potatoes. Follow this with a creamy, milky pudding. If you can, use silver dishes, napkins with an appropriate design and a white tablecloth.

Put fragrant white flowers on the table – use your imagination and make your table as 'lunar' as possible. Light a white candle in the centre if possible in a bowl of water.

Use words of your own choosing, such as:

'Hail to the shining Goddess; may her light fill our nights, our homes and our hearts'.

Each person can have their own say. Women of child-bearing age may wear silver crowns.

Improvise! Have fun!

DE-STRESS
WITH THE
MOON

Life in the fast lane can leave you
strung out. Create a lunar haven in your
home where you can relax and be your
instinctual self. All of these can create a
lunar ambience:

- a fish tank
- silver objects
- goddess figures
- pastels, blues, greens and violets
- plush upholstery and carpets
- an indoor fountain
- prints and paintings of seascapes and the Moon herself
- crystal ornaments
- candles, soft lights
- a tape or CD with sounds of the ocean
- jasmine in an oil-burner

Retreat into your haven when the world has been harsh — but don't overdo it. You need to be able to bring your lunar inspirations back to the everyday world if you are to function.

A LUNAR
SCRAPBOOK

Get in tune with the Moon by making a
lunar scrapbook.

Divide your book into four sections: one
for Dark Moon, one for Waxing Moon,
another for Full Moon and the fourth for
Waning Moon.

Collect pictures and mementoes to stick
in for the four phases. It doesn't matter

whether what you choose seems sensible as long as it feels right to you. For instance, you may wish to stick a picture of an old woman in your Waning Moon section. Some shiny silver coins might go in the Waxing Moon pages. Or Dark Moon might show lots of stars, for these are more visible when the Moon has departed.

Pictures of goddesses and gods can also go in your book, along with poetry, meditations and spells.

Keep your book safe and secret. Use it to get you in the right frame of mind when you do your Moon magic.

AN ALTAR TO
LADY MOON

Create a shrine in your dwelling to the
Queen of the Night. If you need a logical
reason, tell yourself you are getting your
unconscious in tune with natural tides.
Otherwise, just enjoy!

Select a special shelf and cover it
with a silver or white cloth.

Decorate it with silver objects, for silver is the Moon's metal. Animal figures are also suitable and some 'lunar' animals include dolphins, bears, dogs, cats and snakes.

Place candles there. You can choose different colours for the different phases — black for Dark Moon, white for Full Moon, silver for New Moon, blue for Waning Moon.

Figures of goddesses such as Isis or Diana could go on your altar, or the Egyptian Moon-god, Thoth.

Burn a joss-stick to celebrate the Moon:
jasmine for Full Moon,
patchouli for Dark Moon.

Fresh flowers are lovely, or a simple goblet
of water honours the Moon's tidal power.

Don't be afraid to put anything on your
altar that 'feels right' to you.

WANING MOON DETOX

Have you been overdoing it? Feel that
your body is full of toxins? Poisons are
more easily expelled as the Moon wanes,
so work with Doctor Moon and give
yourself a deep cleanse!

Just after Full Moon, cut out meat and dairy produce; drink at least four pints (2 litres) of water per day; eat organic fruits, vegetables and cereals; cut out caffeine and alcohol; exercise for twenty minutes a day and get seven hours sleep per night.

When the next New Moon comes up you too will feel like a new person! Guaranteed!

A MOON RHYME

Modern Nature worshippers revive the old ways and often link their celebrations to the Moon, for she represents the Goddess and shows us the cycle of rebirth in her movements. Here is a chant suitable for many festivals, including lunar ones:

We all come from the Goddess
And to Her we shall return;
Like a drop of rain
Flowing to the ocean.
Hoof and horn, hoof and horn –
All that dies shall be reborn.
Corn and grain, corn and grain –
All that falls shall rise again.
Isis Astarte Diana,
Hecate Demeter Kali
Inanna.

MAIDEN,
MOTHER AND
CRONE

The phases of the Moon depict the three
stages of womanhood. The Maiden is the
Waxing Moon, the Mother the Full Moon
and the Crone the Waning Moon.

Many goddesses are linked with one specific lunar phase and one phase of a woman's life. Equally there are many triple goddesses such as the Three Graces, or groups of three like that of the Greek goddesses Persephone, Demeter and Hecate.

At any age in a woman's life she can make contact with any of the three stages, contacting the wisdom of the Crone, the generosity of the Mother or the freshness of the Maiden — whichever she needs.

Simply use the brilliant Moon as a guide
and light a candle – white for Maiden,
red for Mother, black for Crone.

Meditate, in the Moonlight if possible, and
feel yourself gently absorbing the special
qualities you require as the Moonlight
bathes the sky.

NEW MOON RITUAL TO PERSEPHONE

Persephone is the Maiden goddess who was abducted by the Greek god of the underworld, Pluto, to be his bride. Her mother Demeter, the Earth goddess, created winter in mourning. But the gods decreed that Persephone should return to her mother for half the year and so Spring returns with her.

When you see the first sickle of the New Moon in the sky, light a white candle and burn incense of lavender, lemon peel and parsley. Have two more white candles with you.

Hold up a shiny apple to the Moon or, if you can, use a cut pomegranate instead, for that was the fruit Persephone ate in the Underworld. Say:

'Lady Persephone, as you did eat of the fruit of fertility so do I, embracing all creative change that will come in this cycle.'

Take a bite of the fruit. As you chew, light
the two other candles and say:

'This one is for what I must remember,'
and *'This one is for the future.'*

Re-light the candles each evening until
Full Moon. Bury what you do not eat of
the fruit.

FULL MOON RITUAL

You will need a large bowl, preferably made of silver, and a jasmine joss-stick or incense. If you cannot perform this ritual outside or indoors where the light of the Moon pours in, use either three candles or one large, thick, silver candle as a substitute for the moonlight.

Burn incense. Look at the reflection of the Moon in the water. Say:

'Lady of Dreams, be my inspiration;
Gypsy of the Skies, be my guide;
Queen of the Night, be my protector.'

Drink a little of the water. Immerse your
hands in it, then anoint your face, eyes,
lips, breast, belly, feet and any part of you
that needs healing. If you wish to become
pregnant trace a spiral of the water
around your navel.

Pour any unused water onto the ground.

DARK MOON
RITE TO HECATE

Hecate was a Titaness – a Greek
goddess even older than the Olympian
pantheon. She was goddess of magic
and was believed to stalk the highways
and byways when the Moon was dark.
Crossroads were especially sacred to her.

You will need a black candle; incense
or a joss-stick containing myrrh and/or
patchouli; a black stone such as onyx or

apache tear; a small silver bowl containing water and a white candle.

Light the black candle and hold the stone in your hand. As you look deeply into it, think about the month gone by. Do you wish things had been different? What changes would you like to make? Maybe you are happy with the way it went and want things to continue in the same way. Ask Hecate to give you wisdom and self-knowledge.

When you are ready, wash the black stone in the water, light the white candle from the black and give thanks to Hecate for anything you have realised.

THE MOON RULES

Those who work magic believe in a system of 'correspondences'. This means that if you use substances that 'correspond' to your purpose, your spell will work.

Lunar correspondences include:

COLOURS: white and silver

HERBS AND PLANTS: eucalyptus,
lemon balm, calamus, camellia, camphor,
coconut, lemon, gardenia, grape, jasmine,
lily, lotus, mallow, moonwort, myrrh,
poppy, sandalwood, willow

STONES: pearl, beryl, aquamarine,
crystal, moonstone, sapphire, selenite

METALS: silver

ANIMALS: dog, wolf, dolphin, bear, snake

These correspondences can be used in lunar spells for the home and healing, for children and fertility and for invoking the imagination, intuition, sleep, peace or prophetic dreams. Be creative – combine what you need for your purpose.

All is connected in the cosmic web.

BACH FLOWER REMEDIES

Bach flower remedies involve using delicate solutions of extracted plant material to help emotional problems. Try these Moon-ruled remedies:

WILLOW: to adjust to misfortune and adversity.

ASPEN: to calm vague and unknown fears you are afraid to talk about.

OLIVE: for treating exhaustion or the feeling that life is without pleasure.

VINE: for combating stress, feelings of hardness or callousness and the wish to coerce.

WITCHY
THIRTEEN

Why is thirteen 'unlucky for some' but
connected to witches and magic?

Because the Moon makes thirteen rounds
of the zodiac to one of the Sun, meaning
there are thirteen lunar months in the year.

If you are interested in hidden things
and magic, thirteen could be your lucky
number ...

THE MOON AND THE ZODIAC

Just as the Sun passes through all twelve
signs of the zodiac in one year, so the
Moon passes through them all in less than
a calendar month. It takes the Moon just
under 28 days to travel all the way round
the zodiac. Because the zodiac cycle
of 28 days is less than the Moon-phase
cycle of 29½ days, each month the Full
Moon occurs in the sign following the
previous one.

The sign that the Moon was in when you were born is almost as important as your Sun sign, but to discover your Moon sign you will need to consult special tables or get your birth chart drawn up.

Different sorts of magic may be best undertaken with the Full Moon in a specific sign of the zodiac – however, you don't have to wait if your need is urgent!

THE STRENGTH
OF THE MOON

🌙

The Moon rules the Sun sign of Cancer.
People born under this sign are sensitive,
home-loving and caring.

Those born with the Moon in Cancer in
their horoscope may have very powerful
emotions.

The Moon is exalted in the sign of Taurus.
Those with the Moon in Taurus have
stable, warm feelings and are very faithful
and sensuous.

The Moon is in her detriment in Capricorn, which is opposite Cancer. Those with the Moon in Capricorn may be afraid of their feelings, keeping them locked away.

The Moon is in her fall in Scorpio, which is opposite Taurus. Those with the Moon in Scorpio may have very intense feelings that they find hard to express in a positive manner.

FIRE MOONS

If you were born with the Moon in Aries,
Leo or Sagittarius, you have a fiery Moon.
You are enthusiastic about life and have
great faith in the future – although when
you get depressed everyone knows
about it! You have a sense of fun, love
a bit of drama and you are passionate
and impulsive. To feel 'at home' you need
a sense of warmth, stimulation
and meaning in life.

EARTH MOONS

If you were born with the Moon in Taurus,
Virgo or Capricorn, you have an earthy
Moon. You are rooted in your body and
the evidence of your senses. You like to
be sure of your ground. It takes you a
while to respond but when you do, you
mean it! Sometimes you can be a little
over-cautious. To feel 'at home' you need
security, a sense of control and knowledge
of your resources.

AIR MOONS

If you were born with the Moon in Gemini, Libra or Aquarius, you have an airy Moon. You like to take life lightly and you are very friendly and communicative. You may be quick to respond but you are always just that little bit detached — you aren't keen to get emotionally involved. To feel 'at home' you need to feel free, you need truth and to know all is fair.

WATER MOONS

If you were born with the Moon in Cancer, Scorpio or Pisces, you have a watery Moon. Your feelings run very deep and you do not always find it easy to express them – you like to empathise and to feel people understand and care. You can be very emotional and just a touch manipulative sometimes! To feel 'at home' you need a feeling of belonging, understanding and safety.

ZODIAC SIGNS AND MAGIC

For working magic, the phase of the Moon is generally more important than the sign of the zodiac she occupies. And, although it's easy to check lunar phases in a newspaper, you will need an ephemeris (a list of planetary tables) to know which sign of the zodiac she is in. However, it's easy to work out what sign of the zodiac the Full Moon is in, because she is always in the sign opposite to that occupied by the Sun. All you need to know is the current Sun sign, look at the zodiac wheel and work from that.

If you want to give your magic some extra oomph, work it when the Full Moon is in a good sign for your purpose. But be adaptable! For instance, if you want more mental energy, why wait until the Full Moon appears in Gemini? Use the energies of Full Moon in one of the Fire Signs or in Virgo. You can alter your words to fit.

MOON IN ARIES MAGIC

A Full Moon that occurs between September 23rd and October 23rd will be in Aries. Use this time for any magic to do with:

- sports, competition, taking first place
- having exceptional energy
- facing a challenge, overcoming obstacles
- being brave

- starting something completely new, particularly a new academic year
- healing any ills of the head or treating headaches

Light a red candle and burn oil or incense of cedarwood. Say:

'Aries Moon, strong and bright,
Give to me the strength to fight.'

Follow this with words of your own choosing for your particular intent and finish off by repeating the rhyme three times.

MOON IN TAURUS MAGIC

A Full Moon that occurs between October 24th and November 22nd will be in Taurus. Use this time for magic related to:

- attracting wealth and material possessions
- boosting creativity
- enhancing sexuality and sexual attractiveness
- the good things of life
- security and stability or endurance

• helping your garden through the winter months (if you live in the Northern Hemisphere)
• healing connected with the neck and throat
• boosting the immune system

Light a green candle and burn incense or oil of patchouli or rose. Say,

*'Taurus Moon, riding high,
All good things to me draw nigh.'*

Follow this with words specific to your intent and round off your ritual by repeating the rhyme three times.

MOON IN GEMINI MAGIC

A Full Moon that occurs between November 23rd and December 21st will be in Gemini. Use this time of sparkle, bright ideas, jokes, laughter and repartee to:

• bring light and life close to you
as Yuletide approaches
• hold parties
• speed the post, make arrangements,
swap ideas

- improve communication
- chat between friends, neighbours and siblings
- work with impartial and detached thinking
- travel short-distances
- heal the arms, hands and lungs

Light a pale yellow candle and burn incense or oil of lavender. Say:

'Shining Moon in Gemini,
Light and life to me draw nigh.'

Follow this with more specific words of your own and finish off by repeating the rhyme three times.

MOON IN CANCER MAGIC

A Full Moon that occurs between December 22nd and January 20th will be in Cancer. Use this time of helpful, quiet and domestic Moon for:

- all matters to do with family, children, fertility
- nurturing the imagination, dreams
- working with the home, ancestors and tradition

• matters of the sea or safety
• holidays and family times in the Southern Hemisphere
• healing the stomach and breasts, also the lymphatic system

Light a white candle and burn incense or oil of eucalyptus or jasmine. Say:

'Moon in Cancer, pure and white,
Bring me times of true delight.'

Follow this with more specific words connected to your intent and round off by repeating the rhyme three times.

MOON IN LEO
MAGIC

A Full Moon that occurs between January
21st and February 18th will be in Leo.
Use this time for:

- matters concerning power,
leadership, success
- creativity, determination
- affairs of the stage and entertainment
- romantic relationships and issues to do
with children

- boosting or adding zest to late summer
plans in the Southern Hemisphere
- healing the heart and the chest

Light a gold or orange candle and burn
oil or incense of frankincense, cinnamon or
orange. Say:

'Leo Moon, I bow to you:
Give me success in all I do.'

Follow this with specific words about
your intent and finish off by repeating the
rhyme three times.

MOON IN VIRGO MAGIC

A Full Moon that occurs between February 19th and March 20th will be in Virgo. Use this Moon for:

- getting organised
- having a sort-out, tidying, cleaning
- separating the wheat from the chaff
- reviewing what you have achieved
- catching up with small jobs and matters to do with your daily routine

- cleansing and detoxing of all descriptions
- healing the digestive system

Light a green or yellow candle and burn oil or incense of lavender or mimosa. Say:

'Virgo Moon, crystal clear,
All things in their place appear.'

Follow this with specific words about your purpose and complete with three-times repetition of the rhyme.

MOON IN LIBRA
MAGIC

A Full Moon that occurs between March 21st and April 20th will be in Libra. This Moon is good for:

- promoting justice and fairness
- aiding arbitration and conciliation
- resolving breaches and enabling relationships to go smoothly
- partnership or legal matters and also for bonds of love
- helping people air their differences and find agreement

• creating tact, diplomacy and balance
• healing of the kidneys

Light a blue candle and burn incense or
oil of rose or geranium. Say:

*'Moon in Libra, fair to see,
Bring balance, peace and love to me.'*

Complete this with words of your own
choosing specific to your cause
and finish off by repeating the rhyme
three times.

MOON IN SCORPIO MAGIC

🌙

A Full Moon that occurs between April 21st and May 21st will be in Scorpio. Use this Moon for:

- intense emotional matters such as purging guilt, lust or obsession
- keeping things secret
- solving mysteries and getting to the root of things
- concentration and exam revision

• seeing deep within
• dealing with sexual matters
• healing the sexual organs

Light a deep-red candle and burn incense
or oil of myrrh or ginger. Say:

'Scorpio Moon, rising from the Deep,
Help me all my power to keep.'

Finish this off with words appropriate to
your special purpose and complete it by
repeating the rhyme three times.

MOON IN SAGITTARIUS MAGIC

A Full Moon that occurs between May 22nd and June 21st will be in Sagittarius. This Moon is helpful for:

- the acquisition of wisdom and understanding
- adventures, both mental and physical
- travel that truly broadens the mind
- expanding the conceptual horizons and

getting the 'big picture'
* long-term planning
* 'rising above' spirituality
* long-distance journeys
* healing arthritis and other ills in the hips
and thighs

Light a purple candle and burn incense or
oil of clove or sandalwood. Say:

*'Archer Moon in Heaven's height,
Help my soul now to take flight.'*

Finish this off with specific words for your
purpose and repeat the rhyme three times
to complete the spell.

MOON IN CAPRICORN MAGIC

A Full Moon that occurs between June 22nd and July 22nd will be in Capricorn. This Moon is useful for:

- career matters
- anything to do with status or the establishment of a reputation
- map-reading, planning and organising
- binding and grounding

- containing or ending
- doing what is necessary without becoming emotionally incapable
- healing of the knees

Light a dark blue candle and burn incense or oil of cypress or patchouli. Say:

'Capricorn Moon, bright and round,
Keep my feet upon the ground.'

Follow this with special words for your purpose and finish off by repeating the rhyme three times.

MOON IN AQUARIUS MAGIC

A Full Moon that occurs between July 23rd and August 23rd will be in Aquarius. This Moon is for wishes to come true and it can help with:

- creating detachment
- inspiration and keeping a broad, unbiased outlook
- humanitarian and charitable matters

- telepathy and mental ingenuity
- expanding a social circle and getting together with friends
- healing problems with the ankles

Light a bright blue candle and burn incense or oil of lavender or pine. Say:

*'High Moon in Aquarius,
Grant me something marvellous!'*

Now follow this with specific words of your choosing and finish the spell by repeating the rhyme three times.

MOON IN PISCES MAGIC

A Full Moon that occurs between August 24th and September 22nd will be in Pisces. This psychic Moon helps with:

- the expansion of consciousness
- mysticism and understanding dreams – or dreaming true
- divination and clairvoyance
- escapism and 'getting away from it all'
- feeling laid back and relaxed
- boosting the imagination

• healing of the feet or matters involving bodily fluid balance

Light a violet or turquoise candle and burn incense or oil of ylang-ylang, eucalyptus or sage. Say:

'Moon in Pisces, bright your beam,
Bring to me my sweetest dream.'

Finish this off with words appropriate to your specific purpose and complete the spell by repeating the rhyme three times.

LOOKING INTO THE FUTURE

If you want to become a seer the Moon
can lead you!

Take a large, deep bowl of water and
sit with it between your legs, with the
reflection of the Moon falling in it.

Burn a jasmine joss-stick, but all around
you should be in darkness.

Take a deep breath, close your eyes and
frame your question, clearly and simply.

Open your eyes and stare at the Moon in the water. Look deep, deep within, at the shining, mysterious Moon.

The water may cloud over and you may see figures form. Or you may go into a dreamy state and pictures may form inside your head.

Be sure to take note of everything you see, but do not try to work it out – just watch.

Later on you will be able to interpret and find your answer!

LUNAR
LIBROMANCY

Need a quick answer to a question? There
is a very simple way to divine.
All you need is a book and the influence
of the Moon's phase.

Choose a general book that covers plenty
of life-areas — poetry is good, or a child's
encyclopedia.

If your question is about outer matters
such as 'Does he/she love me?' or 'Which

career path should I take?', choose the
time of Full Moon to ask the oracle.
If your question is an inward one about
knowing yourself and your feelings,
such as:

'Am I really happy here?' or 'Can I really
trust ... ?', choose Dark Moon.

Close your eyes, hold the book on your
lap and let the pages run past your
fingers, until you feel like stopping.

Open your eyes and the first phrase you
see on the page will hold your answer.

BOOST YOUR INTUITION

Intuition is a natural thing! Candles and incantations are fine, but we develop true contact with our instincts by spending time in the places where they are really at home – in nature.

If you want to deepen your understanding and develop as a seer, take regular walks when the Moon is in the sky. Look at her, watch her in all her moods and phases. See how the world looks when bathed in

the silver glow of Full Moon. Touch trees
to see how they 'feel' at Full Moon. Watch
the way animals and birds behave and
be aware of the resonance of the earth
beneath your feet.

Let your inner eye open in response
to the Moon!

A LUNAR
BOUQUET

Gather an armful of fragrant Moon
flowers to celebrate Full Moon. Include
lilies, camellia, gardenia, jasmine, poppies
and some sprigs of willow if you can.
All or any will do – include other white
flowers if you like. (Although roses are
strictly ruled by Venus, white roses may
have lunar links).

Smell the fragrance and draw the subtle
beauty of the Moon within you.

Arrange the flowers on your altar, or place
in a shaded corner of your room, to invite
the Moon inside.

MOON RUNES

In ancient times an alphabet was much
more than a collection of sounds. People
understood that all is vibration and that in
the cosmic spectrum everything is linked.
So alphabets had magical meanings.

The Runic alphabet was used by the
Vikings and its symbols were revered.
Two runes in this alphabet had strong
connections with the Moon:

ALGIZ ⟨Y⟩ links with the yew tree and with the qualities of protection, meditation and healing. Meditating upon it can give you insight. Focussing on it can help your career, creativity and friendship and put you in charge of your emotions.

OTHILA ⟨ᛟ⟩ links with the hawthorn and with your home and property. Meditating upon it can help you feel that you belong, and help you put down roots. Focussing on it is good for marriage and children as well as for connecting with your spiritual heritage.

MOON NUMBERS

Ancient people – and modern numerologists! – believe that numbers do not just convey quantity. They also have a 'quality', a vibrational signature, forming part of the cosmic web that surrounds us.

The number 2 is lunar, for the Moon is the second brightest light in the sky after the Sun and in her phases the Moon has two horns. The ancients believed that 2 was a very feminine, receptive number, sometimes subtle and scheming but very sweet and even-tempered.

Each of us has several important personal numbers. You can discover yours by: adding together the digits of your birthday (e.g. for the 29th = 2+9 = 11 = 1+1 = 2) adding up the digits of your entire birth date (i.e. the numbers of the month, day and year) the numerical correspondences of your name (each letter can be converted to a number, starting with A = 1 etc. up to I = 9, and then starting with J = 1 again).

Do you have many 2s in your numerical make-up? Then you are a gentle Lunarian. Any 2s in your address or phone number will bring co-operation and domestic balance.

LUNAR
ALCHEMY

🌙

Alchemy was popular in the Middle Ages
and lots of mysterious diagrams and
writings on the subject survive, many of
which include lunar symbols. Alchemy was
more than an attempt to turn base metals
into gold — it was a spiritual quest.

The alchemist's power came from the
conjunctio — the union of the King and the
Queen. The King was symbolised by the

Sun, the Queen by the Moon. This is a reminder to look deep within ourselves, to the balance of male and female, yin and yang, inside. Without balance there can be no creativity; without true awareness of ourselves there can be no progress.

Let the Moon teach you to look within, as she has taught so many through the centuries.

THE MOON IN THE TAROT

The Tarot can be used for divination and for self-development. In the Tarot, the Moon is card number 15 of the Major Arcana and it is associated with the astrological sign of Pisces.

The card may appear in any of a multitude of designs, depending on the deck, but it will always show the Moon and may display other associated images such as the sea, baying dogs or other lunar creatures.

In a spread, the Moon card can mean
illusion, confusion and self-deception.
However, reflecting upon this card can help
you to develop psychism, increase your
awareness of dream meanings and your
connection with natural rhythms. It triggers
an ability to 'go with the flow' and to be
aware of our roots in the time before time,
when instincts were strong.

To make contact with your inner wisdom,
and to avoid the self-deception that this
card can imply, prop the Moon card
where you can see it while you meditate.
Light a purple candle and let your
awareness deepen.

THE MOON IN YOUR HAND

The mounts on the hand denote certain characteristics and are named after the planets.

The Mount of Luna, or the Moon, is found towards the outside of the palm, just above the wrist, opposite the thumb.

If the mount is high and well-formed, the intuition, imagination and psychic faculties are likely to be pronounced.

These characteristics will be even more prominent if a star formation or other special marking appears on this mount.

The Line of Intuition – when present – encircles the mount and signifies marked psychic and mediumistic ability.

Where the Head Line (the lower of the two main lines that cross the palm) bends down toward the Mount of Luna, logic gives way before the emotions – guard against depression and illusion and follow your heart.

MOON ANGEL

The angel of the Moon is Gabriel, whose
name means 'Strength of God'.

This archangel is a messenger, awakening
us to cosmic truth and appears many
times in the Bible as a harbinger of
creative change. Gabriel also parted
the waters of the Red Sea so that the
Hebrews could escape from Egypt,
suggesting a connection with the tides
and with passage. Islamic tradition states
that Gabriel, being the Angel of Truth,
revealed the Koran to Mohammed.

Often depicted holding a lily — which is ruled by the Moon — or a sceptre, this angel may be male or female. S/he brings the gifts of psychism, seeing and hearing, fertility and balance. Gabriel comes to us in dreams, whispering those special things we need to know.

Invoke Gabriel with incense or oils of jasmine and/or mimosa and by wearing a fire opal.

WILLOW LORE

The willow is ruled by the Moon.
Willow roots will often extend far
underground in search of water.

This lunar tree is sacred to the Chinese
goddess of compassion, Kuan Yin, who
uses a willow branch to sprinkle the waters
of life.

The willow also signifies death, which is
part of the cycle of re-growth.

The tree is also associated with rejection in love. The custom of wearing the green willow around a hat when love is lost may originate from a charm against the jealousy of the Moon goddess. The Moon is about emotions that may be changeable and fickle and also about the ways in which we may deceive ourselves. But on the other hand, if you want to attract love, carry a willow-leaf!

Willow bark and sandalwood may be burnt together as incense under a waning Moon to call up spirits.

A NEW BROOM

The plant broom *(cytisus scoparius)* is said by some to be ruled by the Moon. Witches use a besom made from this plant for sweeping out their circle in ritual cleansing, before magic.

It was the plant behind the heraldic design of the Plantagenet family, who were said to be involved in the magical arts.

If you are plagued by poltergeists and restless spirits, make an infusion of broom by steeping the plant substances in hot water — the proportions are not crucial. Sprinkle this around your property, saying,

> *'Plant of broom so strong,*
> *Rid me of all that's wrong,*
> *Keep me and mine safe and sound,*
> *By your magic all around.'*

INCENSE

You do not have to use incense but it often helps to create the right atmosphere for spells if you do.

For your Moon rites, choose a silver censer or heat-proof dish for your incense (*do not use* an old ashtray as this will not be strong enough).

Obtain charcoal discs from a New Age shop. Hold one in tongs, against a flame, until it sparks and begins to go grey. Lay the disc flat in your censer and sprinkle your incense in the centre.

A New Moon blend can contain lavender, lemon balm and calamus.

A Full Moon blend can contain frankincense, sandalwood and rose (petals or essence).

A Waning/Dark Moon blend can contain myrrh, cypress, copal and/or Orris root.

THE OLIVE TREE

The olive is sacred to the Moon and
Gabriel, the angel of the Moon, is often
shown with an olive branch.

Greek brides wore a crown of olives for
fertility and olive leaves can be scattered
to bring peace and tranquillity.

The olive leaf symbolises the renewal of
life. Carry an olive leaf for luck and share
olives with your lover, for they are an
aphrodisiac!

MAGIC
MONDAY

Monday is the 'Moon's Day' – that is the origin of the name. This is also true in French, *Lundi* being the day of *la lune*.

Monday is the traditional day for spells for love and togetherness, for healing hurts, family matters, gardening, travel, anything to do with water or the sea and for 'the sight'.

The third hour after sunset is the best time for rituals.

If the Full Moon falls on, or just after Monday, this is an especially powerful occasion magically.

MAGIC CIRCLE

All magic is best performed inside a
ritual circle, which gives protection and
concentration.

For your Moon magic, make your circle
by directing energy with your forefinger,
clockwise, in a circle around you. Visualise
it as blue light.

Your circle should be guarded by the four
Elemental Powers at the four quarters.
These powers are associated with lunar
phases:

NORTH is Earth and Dark Moon.
Light a black candle.
EAST is Air and Waxing Moon.
Light a silver candle.
SOUTH is Fire and Full Moon.
Light a red or white candle.
WEST is Water and Waning Moon.
Light a blue candle.

Now you have the symbolic presence of
all the phases and elements to strengthen
any rite. Always mentally dismantle your
circle when you have finished and give
thanks.

(N.B In the Southern hemisphere, swap
the North/South elements and phases and
move anti-clockwise when creating your
circle.)

LUNAR
TOGETHERNESS

Have you and your other half been going
through a hard time lately? Let the Moon
bring you close again.

When the Moon is full, fill a large bowl
with fresh water. Add some drops of rose
or jasmine oil, or float white rose-petals on
top.

Let the Full Moon reflect in the water as you both sit near the bowl. Put your hands in it, play with the water and with each other's fingers. Hold hands, caress, say nothing ...

Now begin gently to trace the Moon-water over the face of your lover – forehead, eyes, lips. Linger as long as you like, then progress to other parts of the body.

No need for words – let your fingers do the talking!

TRAVELLER'S MOON

The Moon is a wanderer, but she always returns.

If you have to go far away from home for any length of time, try this spell to keep you safe and attached to your roots.

You will need a length of cord, seven silver beads, seven white beads and a large silver candle.

Starting at New Moon, light your candle
in the evening and thread one white
bead on your cord, naming something
good about your home that you want to
retain. The next night thread a silver bead,
naming it for something you hope to gain
from your travel. Continue alternately with
each evening that follows.

At Full Moon thread your last silver bead
and knot the cord round your candle. Let
it burn down.

Keep your cord-charm with you as you
roam — you will never be far from home.

LUNAR
HEALING

Healing magic is a lunar province.

To send someone well-being, ask their
permission to help. Choose a Waxing
Moon to work this charm. Anoint a green
candle with eucalyptus oil or ring it with
a eucalyptus wreath. Imagine the person
smiling and joyful. Say:

'As the shining Moon does swell,
So may ⟨name⟩ be happy and well.'

You may do this each evening until Full
Moon. Then, why not raise a glass of wine
or grape juice to the Moon in thanks —
along with your fully-recovered friend!

LUNAR LUCK

Know when the New Moon is due to arrive? It is especially lucky to see it for the first time over your right shoulder.

Look out for the first New Moon in the New Year. When you see it, speak your wish out loud — it will be fulfilled.

The first Full Moon is lucky too — it will make your wish materialise before the year ends.

TO SEE YOUR TRUE LOVE

Wait for the first Full Moon of the New Year. Go out to where the reflection of the Moon falls on a pool or stretch of water.

Look for your reflection there. Allow yourself to feel relaxed and dreamy. The face of your future love will be reflected back at you, beside your own.

WISHING MOON

Write your wish on a bay-leaf when the Moon is new. (The writing doesn't have to be clear or detailed – initials will do, as long as *you are* very clear about your wish.)

Hold the leaf to your forehead while you look at the Moon, imagining your wish materialising.

Sleep with the bay leaf under your pillow.

TO DETER TROUBLESOME NEIGHBOURS

Take a small hand-mirror and leave it out
in the light of the Full Moon for several
nights until the Moon has started to wane.
(N.B: it does not matter if the Moon is
behind cloud for much of the time, as long
as it has been caught in Moonlight at
least once.)

Hold the mirror in your right hand and say:

'Trouble, come is trouble turned –
Peace and love to all concerned.'

Place the mirror on a windowsill, facing
towards your nasty neighbours. Relax!
Your shield is in place!

TO FIND A NEW HOME

When you see the first silver crescent in the sky, light a white candle that you have anointed with a little lavender oil. Visualise all the things you want in your new home. Say:

'Moon, as you sail o'er Heaven's dome,
Spy for me a lovely home
Where I can be happy, where I can rest.
O Wandering Moon, now do your best!'

Light the candle every night until the Moon is full. Repeat next month, if necessary.

TO BREAK A
CURSE

In fact, the vast majority of 'curses' exist
only in the mind of the one 'cursed'
by reason of their own negativity.
Nonetheless, this will help ...

Choose the first Saturday of the waning
Moon and light a black candle. Say:

'I return all that is dark and evil to this black candle. As it burns down so will all that is harmful to me burn away and be destroyed. Ashes to ashes, dust to dust, so mote it be.'

Burn each night until the candle is gone and/or the Moon has disappeared from the sky. Bury any leftover wax in the garden.

MONEY MOON

There are many lunar spells you can do to attract wealth.

When the Moon is new, place a bank-note of the largest sum you afford underneath the doormat at your front door. Remove it only when the Moon is full and return it there at the next New Moon if you like. The larger the bank-note the greater the dividend – and the more feet that walk over it the better!

Alternatively, place as much money as you can on your windowsill in the light of the New Moon. Say:

'O magic Moon, make my money grow.'

You can repeat this also at the next New Moon.

FOLK SPELL
FOR MONEY

When you see the very first silver sickle –
not through glass – turnover the silver
coins in your pocket and say:

*'In the name of the Great Mother,
the Horned God and the Magical Child,
may my money grow this month!'*

Now fortune is on its way!

MOONWORT
MONEY SPELLS

This herb is ruled by the Moon. Place a
sprig of moonwort in your purse to attract
more silver.

Place it in a box at the back of your
cupboard and wealth will come to you.

Burn dried moonwort at the New Moon.
Watch the vapours rise and imagine the
wealth that will soon be yours.

SANDALWOOD
SPELLS

Fragrant sandalwood is ruled by the
Moon. It is used as incense especially for
spells for healing, protection and exorcism.
Mix with frankincense for a Full Moon rite.

Take a large chip of sandalwood and
write a wish on it. Burn this in a heat-proof
dish, visualising your wish as you do so, to
make it come true.

Wear beads made of sandalwood for
protection and spiritual development.
Leave them in the light of the Full Moon
occasionally, for extra power.

WILLOW
WEDDING?

Moon-ruled willow can give you an
answer about your love life. To find out
if you will have a relationship over the
coming year, throw your shoe into a willow
tree. You can have nine tries in all and if
your shoe catches you will be with your
love by the end of the next year.

Give this a try at a party next New Year's
Eve — but remember, you're going to have
to climb that tree to get your shoe back!

WATCHFUL WINTERGREEN

Wintergreen is a Moon herb and will protect children if a little is placed inside their pillow case. It can bring them life-long good fortune.

Mix it with mint and sprinkle around the house to remove bad vibes.

COCONUT NICE!

Coconut is ruled by the Moon. Your home will remain safe if you hang a coconut in it. But if you don't fancy this hairy ornament, then cut a coconut in two, drain it and fill the inside with a selection of protective herbs such as clove, frankincense, rosemary, mint and eucalyptus. Seal it back up and bury it in the garden.

WORKPLACE
MAGIC

Fed up with the rat-race? Would you prefer to be at home, where it's safe and peaceful? The Moon understands.

Find yourself a clear crystal. Place it out, or on your windowsill, in the light of the Full Moon. Ask the Moon for calmness, serenity and for protection from back-biting and office politics.

Next morning take your crystal to work and put it on your desk. Take a minute to recall the peace of the Full Moon. Imagine your charged-up crystal is projecting a force-field around you, like a crystal egg, shielding you from negativity. Then get on with your work in peace.

Recharge your crystal at each Full Moon.

WANING MOON SPELL FOR JUSTICE

Is someone treating you unfairly or trying to make you go against your beliefs? Do this spell at the Waning Moon.

Make a circle of sage leaves, dried or fresh. In the middle place something that symbolises the subject matter, such as a coin for money, ring for partnership, model house for property, etc.

Sprinkle some sage onto your symbol and follow with a sprinkle of lavender drops for wisdom and clear communication. Bind the symbol round and round with black thread, seeing your resentment and all the troubles being 'bound up' along with it.

Leave this on your window-ledge until the first crescent of the Moon appears. Take it outside and unbind it, seeing all the negative issues take flight. Bury the cord in the ground along with your symbol — or if this is to be used again, wash it in a running stream. Go forward with a clear head and light heart.

SALT SPELL FOR PROTECTION

The Moon-ruled sea is salty and salt has many ritual uses involving cleansing and protecting.

Fill a clear vessel with spring water and leave it out in full sunlight and the light of the waxing Moon for a twenty-four hour period.

Now dissolve some salt in the water.

Sprinkle this in the four corners of the room that needs to be protected. Sprinkle it also around the window and door.

If you need to protect an entire apartment, house and garden, sprinkle the mixture round the boundaries.

LUNAR LOVE
SPELL

When the New Moon appears in the sky
find a heart-shaped petal, preferably of
a rose.

You will need some red or rose-pink paper
and a silver pen. Write on the paper:

'As the fair Moon waxes to full,
My true love to me I pull.'

Have a bath or shower and put on a
clean robe – or stand naked.

Light a rose-red candle and chant your
words three times, while you hold the
petal in the candle-glow.

Fold the paper round the petal and seal
it with some of the wax from the candle.
Place the paper somewhere safe.

By the time New Moon arrives again, love
should have come too.

BEAUTY AND
THE BATH

Need a special boost for an
important date?

Choose the time when the Moon is just
approaching full. Light six candles in silver
holders around your bath. Three candles
should be rose pink, three white.
The bathroom should be warm.

Drop some rose oil and/or sprinkle rose petals onto the surface of the bath water. Burn a rose-scented joss-stick, or place more of the oil in an oil burner.

Soft, sensuous music will help you relax. Close your eyes and imagine that your body is absorbing radiant beauty from the surrounding water. Just feel yourself glow! Imagine as many seductive situations as possible, where the lover of your dreams is totally smitten by you.

When you are ready to get out, wrap yourself a huge, soft, rose-coloured towel and get ready in a leisurely way, knowing that delights are to come!

ANGER BEGONE!

Choose a Waning Moon for this spell and, if you can, stay up until you can see the Waning Moon in the sky.

Burn a black candle. Write down all the things that are making you angry on a piece of white paper with a black pen. Get it all out! Then twist the paper into a taper. Think of how good it will be to be free of these thoughts.

Light the paper in the candle flame and place it in a strong dish – preferably black – to burn.

Carefully take the ashes out and cast them at the Waning Moon, saying:

*'Old Moon, on the wane
Take away my ire and pain.'*

Sprinkle a little lavender oil on your pillow and imagine all the good things to come as you fall asleep.

WHITE WASH

Are you dashing around too much, not giving yourself time to think, feeling cut-off, confused and stressed?

When the Moon is full and fair, take a white satin scarf out into the moonlight. Hold it resting on your arms. Face the Moon and close your eyes.

Feel the light of the Moon wash through you, cleansing away all the stress, muddles and anxiety. Let your mind go blank, breathe deeply and take the lunar glow deep inside you, opening your mind, making you calm and receptive.

Drape the scarf about you, come back inside, have a milky drink and wind down — do nothing for the rest of the evening.

Wear the white scarf whenever you need to chill. Recharge it with the same ritual next Full Moon, if you need to.

FAERIES BY MOONLIGHT

The Irish know faeries as 'the People
of the *Sidhe'* – beautiful and terrible
creatures from another dimension. It is a
great privilege to see faeries: do not be
afraid but be very respectful.

One of the favourite traditional times to see faeries is by the light of the Full Moon. When the Full Moon shines on the trees of the Faery Triad – the oak and ash and thorn – then you may be especially likely to glimpse the Fair Folk.

A garden full of fragrant roses is sure to appeal to faeries – look for them at midnight by the light of the Moon.

But if you fear to see the Little People when you have to go abroad when the Full Moon is gleaming then carry a sprig of gorse for protection.

MOON STONE
~ BERYL

Crystal balls used to be made of this
Moon-ruled stone.

Beryl can be worn to keep you safe
when travelling by sea. It guards against
drowning and also against sea-sickness.

Wearing beryl can help you resist
manipulation and coercion by salesmen
and evangelists.

Five hundred years ago, it was believed that beryl could help the wearer to win debates and still be liked and respected by all!

Beryl is exchanged by lovers so that their love may remain true.

MOON STONE
~ CHALCEDONY

This milky white stone is ruled by the
Moon.

It brings peace, calms fears and cheers
the heart, when held or worn.

It wards off black magic and all negativity.

It is especially useful for nursing mothers,
who can wear beads of chalcedony to
help stimulate the flow of milk.

MOON STONE
~ CRYSTAL

There are many types of crystal and it is, of course, the favourite substance for the 'crystal ball' although balls for divination can also be made of glass or of other stones such as amethyst. White, clear crystal is especially powerful for Moon magic, especially when set within silver.

To make your own miniature circle of
power, choose a variety of white crystals
and embed them in white or silver sand in
a large dish. Or, if you are quite sure of
your final design, you could set them in
self-hardening modelling clay.

For your design, you could set the crystals
in the pattern of astrological symbols such
as a crescent for the Moon or the 'female'
sign of a circle with a cross beneath
for Venus. Or just do whatever feels
right for you.

Use your crystal temple to 'charge' objects
that you are going to use magically, such
as charms and amulets. For instance,
a piece of rose quartz set within the
Venus sign and left out in the Full Moon
would make a wonderful love charm.

MOON STONE
~ GEODES

All crystals take shape within geodes,
which are hollow, often egg-shaped
structures that may be very beautiful.
They may be quite expensive, but make
wonderful ornaments and magical objects.

Keep a geode in your bedroom while
making love if you want to have a baby,
but take it out before sleeping, as crystals
can be powerful things.

Use a special geode as a focus for meditation, catching the flickering candle-glow — amethyst is especially good for this — or place one on your altar to amplify your energies when doing magic. A geode on a lunar altar is a perfect way to honour Lady Moon.

MOON STONE
~ MARBLE

Marble is made of lime and shares some similarities with coral. Marble is a protective substance. Place some marble on your altar if you are doing spells to shield you from attack of any sort, or carry a piece that you have 'charged up' by either leaving it in the light of the Full Moon or in a magical rite.

Marble is good for kitchen fittings as it brings the right lunar 'vibe' for cookery, domestic arts and security. Work surfaces with a marble finish aren't quite the same, so add a real marble chopping board for greater effect.

MOON STONE~ AQUAMARINE

This blue-green stone has links with the sea.

Leave an aquamarine in a clear glass of fresh spring water in the light of the Full Moon for several hours. Take out the stone with clean fingers and sip the water to cleanse you inwardly and to prepare you for magic or divination.

MOON STONE ~ MOONSTONE

Obviously with strong lunar associations, moonstone's powers are so linked to its namesake that these gems are said to wax and wane with the Moon in the heavens.

Moonstone is sacred to the Moon goddess and many witches like to wear it. It can be placed beneath your pillow for a restful sleep and sweet dreams, or a moonstone necklace can be worn in bed.

It is also protective and can be given to your friends when they go off on a trip, especially if travelling by sea.

Hold the stone in your hand as the Moon is waxing to full. Visualise the lunar power as a white light that beams down, surrounding the little stone and causing it to pulsate with protective energy. So great is the survival power of this little stone that the bearer cannot possibly come to harm!

Give it with love – and ask for a postcard in return!

MOON STONE
~ MOTHER-OF-
PEARL

This isn't really a 'stone' but the interior
of the shells of sea molluscs. Avoid
commercial mother-of-pearl because the
creatures will have been killed to obtain it.
Collect your own, if possible, in rock-pools
and streams.

Empower a special piece of mother-of-pearl to give as a protective gift for a newborn baby – or you could simply use a clean sea-shell.

When the first silver sickle appears in the sky, face the Moon, hold up your piece of mother-of-pearl and visualise the sparkling light entering it.
Feel it tingling with power. Say:

*'New Moon, as you grow and shine,
so may this little one grow and thrive.
Blessed Be.'*

Give it, wrapped in white satin, to the parents.

MOON METAL ~ SILVER

Silver has long been sacred to the Moon. Witches and priestesses often wore silver crescents in honour of the lunar Goddess.

Silver reflects negativity away from the person who wears it, just as the Moon reflects the light of the Sun. The 'horns' of a silver crescent repel evil.

Silver is related to love, healing the emotions and psychic abilities. Wearing silver may attract love, but can cause you to feel emotionally overwhelmed at the time of the Full Moon – when wearing gold can balance its effect.

Silver set with a stone ruled by the Moon is a powerful lunar charm. Those touched by silver are able to shed anger and nervousness. A silver ring can keep you calm.

Silver jewellery helps you sleep, especially if set with moonstone. It can give you psychic dreams. Silver may also be placed beneath the pillow for the same effect. This metal also guards travellers, especially those at sea.

TO GET RID OF
A PROBLEM

When the Moon is waning, write your
problem on a piece of paper and burn it.
Simple!

TO END A RUN
OF BAD LUCK

Check the Moon phases in a calendar
or diary and time this spell so the last
day you do it falls on the last day of the
waning Moon. Each day go for a walk
and pick up a piece of dried wood. Do
this for seven days. When the Moon is
at her darkest, bind the twigs with black
thread and burn them. Say:

'Ill luck, your time has come to die;
A bright new phase is drawing nigh.'

LUNAR LAW OF MAGIC

Moon will wane and Moon will grow:
'Harm none' is the one rule you must
know!